MW01040020

THE *Illuminated* CATECHISM

DOODLE • JOURNAL • REFLECT

Written by
Tony Cook

Illustrations by
Susan Spellman

CONCORDIA PUBLISHING HOUSE • SAINT LOUIS

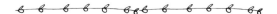

Special thanks to my son, Ben,
who helped make this illustrated
catechism possible.

Published by Concordia Publishing House
3558 S. Jefferson Ave., St. Louis, MO 63118–3968
1-800-325-3040 • cph.org

Text copyright © 2017 Tony Cook. Illustrations copyright © 2017 Concordia Publishing House.

All rights reserved. No part of this publication may be reproduced, stored in a retrieval system, or transmitted, in any form or by any means, electronic, mechanical, photocopying, recording, or otherwise, without the prior written permission of Concordia Publishing House.

Catechism quotations are taken from *Luther's Small Catechism with Explanation,* copyright © 1986, 1991 Concordia Publishing House.
All rights reserved.

Unless otherwise indicated, Scripture quotations are from the ESV® Bible (The Holy Bible, English Standard Version®), copyright © 2001 by Crossway, a publishing ministry of Good News Publishers. Used by permission. All rights reserved.

Except for those noted below, hymn texts with the abbreviation *LSB* are from *Lutheran Service Book*, copyright © 2006 Concordia Publishing House. All rights reserved.

LSB 859 © 1982 Concordia Publishing House. *LSB* 817 © 1968 Augsburg Publishing House. *LSB* 540 © 2001 Steven P. Mueller.
LSB 620 © David Rogner. *LSB* 581:5 and 766:2–5, 7 © 1980 Concordia Publishing House. All hymns used by permission of copyright holders.

Hymn text with the abbreviation *LW* is from *Lutheran Worship*, copyright © 1982 by Concordia Publishing House. All rights reserved.

Hymn text with the abbreviation *TLH* is from *The Lutheran Hymnal*, copyright © 1941 by Concordia Publishing House. All rights reserved.

Except for the hymn noted below, hymn texts with the abbreviation *ELH* are from *Evangelical Lutheran Hymnary*, copyright © 1996
by The Evangelical Lutheran Synod. Used by permission.

ELH 243 is from *Hymns and Hymn Writers of Denmark* © 1945 Committee on Publication of the Danish Evangelical Lutheran Church in America.
Used by permission of Augsburg Fortress.

The quotations marked AE are from the American Edition of Luther's Works: volumes 1–30 © 1955–76 and volumes 58–60, 67–69,
75–78 © 2009–15 Concordia Publishing House; volumes 31–54 © 1957–86 Augsburg Fortress.

The explanation of Luther's Rose on page 88 is from Martin Luther's Letter to Lazarus Spengler, July 8, 1530 (WA Br 5:445);
tr. P. T. McCain © 2016 Concordia Publishing House.

Art on pages 5, 9, 17, 45, 57, 65, 73, 75, © Shutterstock, Inc.

Manufactured in the United States of America
1 2 3 4 5 6 7 8 9 10   25 24 23 22 21 20 19 18 17

THIS CATECHISM ILLUMINATED
BY

. . . .

FOREWORD

Instruction in the basics of the Christian faith plays a vital role in creating a grounded, resilient Christian community. A well-educated Christian is able to share the faith with those outside the Church as well as defend the faith from attacks and confusion. Over the years, the method of basic instruction in the faith has included personal tutoring, sermons, and—with the advent of the printing press—posters, pamphlets, and books such as the Small Catechism. Many early printed catechisms contained beautiful woodcuts that illustrated the catechism's content.

Martin Luther's Small Catechism follows in the Church's rich tradition of Christian instruction. Luther first wrote his Small Catechism in 1529. He designed the brief work to be used in the home as a tool to strengthen the faith of Christian families. Luther believed the Small Catechism contained the basics of the Christian faith. He divided his Small Catechism into Six Chief Parts: The Ten Commandments, The Creed, The Lord's Prayer, The Sacrament of Holy Baptism, Confession, and The Sacrament of the Altar. The text followed a question and answer format that when spoken aloud created a back and forth conversation between the parent and the child.

Even though Luther's catechism is small in size, the depth of its material provides for a lifetime of reflection and serves as a faithful companion for all ages.

welcome

Traditionally, illuminated manuscripts were the result of countless hours of work by an artist who would beautifully illustrate pages of Scripture or a devotional text with decorative lettering, borders, and drawings. These colorful additions to the text enticed the eye and sparked the imagination, but above all, they focused the reader to meditate on the sacred texts. The majority of illuminated manuscripts stem from the Middle Ages and Renaissance. Creating them was a complex and costly process reserved for the wealthy; thus they were, and continue to be, available to very few.

However, this *Illuminated Catechism* is yours. The words printed on these pages comprise only part of the work. While you will find selections from Luther's Small Catechism, Bible passages, and short devotional thoughts, there is also empty space—space for your doodling, journaling, and reflection. Each portion of this catechism includes an illustration designed to provide additional "space" for reflection on the catechetical teaching. As you color each illustration, take time to contemplate and pray about what you read. Before you know it, you will have spent many relaxing hours reflecting on God's grace, praying, and deepening your understanding of the Christian faith. You will become the artist of a unique and beautifully illuminated manuscript, but the time spent in devotional reflection is the true work of art.

"You should meditate, that is, not only in your heart, but also externally, by actually repeating and comparing oral speech and literal words of the book, reading and rereading them with diligent attention and reflection, so that you may see what the Holy Spirit means by them." —LUTHER (AE 34:286)

Regarding the book itself, the paper was selected to allow you to color the illustrations, record your reflections, and doodle in the margins. Feel free to use the artistic tools that best fit your style. If you select a water-based medium or artistic markers, test the ink to see if it bleeds through the page. My personal preference is to use blendable colored pencils. However, while I offer these suggestions on how to use this catechism, there is no one right way. The best way is to make it your own.

Blessings on your journey,

Tony Cook

What does it mean for you to cling, cleave, and trust in God?

COME, THOU FOUNT OF EV'RY BLESSING, TUNE MY HEART TO SING THY GRACE;

THE FIRST COMMANDMENT

YOU SHALL HAVE NO OTHER GODS.

What does this mean? We should fear, love, and trust in God above all things.

The heart is a clinging vine—persistently creeping, seeking a sustaining source. When the source is found, it clings—attaching itself with bonds of trust and devotion. God desires to be our sustaining source, an eternal fountain gushing forth nothing but good. "Whatever you lack," God says, "expect it of Me." "Cling to Me and I will provide." "Do not let your heart cling to another." The desire of God's heart is that our heart's desires be found in Him and Him alone.

The First Commandment teaches us about God's promise of provision; it is a covenant between the source of all good things and the creation God made. It is a call to trust in God alone. It is a call to seek His blessings, to seek them in and through His creation, in and through His creatures, but to never confuse the good we receive with the source of all that is good. In this commandment, God invites us to cling, cleave, and trust in Him, to securely attach ourselves with all our heart to Him, the trustworthy source.

Every good gift and every perfect gift is from above, coming down from the Father of lights, with whom there is no variation or shadow due to change. (JAMES 1:17)

STREAMS OF MERCY, NEVER CEASING, CALL FOR SONGS OF LOUDEST PRAISE. (*LSB* 686:1)

How can you bless God's name in prayer?

YOU SHALL NOT MISUSE THE NAME OF THE LORD YOUR GOD.

What does this mean? We should fear and love God so that we do not curse, swear, use satanic arts, lie, or deceive by His name, but call upon it in every trouble, pray, praise, and give thanks.

. . . .

How we use a person's name presents to the world a picture of what we believe about that person's character, qualities, and worth. Our mouth speaks what our heart believes. This is especially true when we speak God's name. God's name is more than a label; it represents who He is and all that He has done. God desires His children to make use of His name—to call upon it, invoke it, and speak it—in a way that is faithful to who He is each and every day of our life.

The Second Commandment teaches us to connect and to call—to connect God's name to all that is good and true; and to call upon His name in moments of prayer, praise, and thanksgiving. To bring God's name "into the service of truth" and to use it in "a blessed way," as Luther wrote in the Large Catechism, is to use it rightly and honor it as holy. In this commandment, God invites us to call Him by name, signifying our relationship to Him and His promise to be our God.

He sent redemption to His people; He has commanded His covenant forever. Holy and awesome is His name! **(PSALM 111:9)**

O BLESS THE LORD, MY SOUL! LET ALL WITHIN ME JOIN AND AID MY TONGUE TO BLESS HIS NAME WHOSE FAVORS ARE DIVINE. **(*LSB* 814:1)**

How can you honor what God has done in your times of rest?

REMEMBER THE SABBATH DAY BY KEEPING IT HOLY.

What does this mean? We should fear and love God so that we do not despise preaching and His Word, but hold it sacred and gladly hear and learn it.

• •

Taking time to rest, reflect, and give honor to all that God has done was first done by God Himself. He then graciously gave this opportunity to rest from our work and reflect on His Word and work to every human, beginning with Adam and Eve. While for many Christians, Sunday is the day dedicated to spending time in God's Word and Christian community, every day of our Christian life is a holy day. Every day is an opportunity to immerse ourselves in the Word of God. For, each time we do, new understandings and deeper devotion are awakened in our mind and heart.

The Third Commandment teaches us to dedicate ourselves to holy things—holy words, holy works, and a holy life. Time spent reading, hearing, and meditating on God's Word; conducting our life in a faithful and God-pleasing way; and using our words and actions in service to others fulfills this commandment in our daily life. In this commandment, God invites us to use our times of rest to remember Him, rest our body, and feed our faith, as we strive to live a life that honors Him.

So then, there remains a Sabbath rest for the people of God, for whoever has entered God's rest has also rested from his works as God did from His. **(HEBREWS 4:9–10)**

TAKE MY LIFE AND LET IT BE CONSECRATED, LORD, TO THEE;

TAKE MY MOMENTS AND MY DAYS, LET THEM FLOW IN CEASELESS PRAISE. **(LSB 783:1)**

What opportunities do you have to honor God by honoring those in authority?

HONOR YOUR FATHER AND YOUR MOTHER.

What does this mean? We should fear and love God so that we do not despise or anger our parents and other authorities, but honor them, serve and obey them, love and cherish them.

. . . .

Parents come in many forms. Some are parents by blood, others by bonds of love, and still others by positions of authority and office. Regardless of their form, parents are people to whom we naturally turn for the good things we need. Parents and authorities are appointed by God to be His representatives in this world. Our relationship with our parents is meant to reflect the relationship God desires to have with all His children regardless of their age, race, or creed. God is the Father of all and our parents are an extension of His parental love.

The Fourth Commandment teaches us that God's authority flows through those whom He has appointed—beginning with our parents. When we honor our father and mother, we are acknowledging not only their position but also God who is working through them. To honor our parents is to honor God. This divinely given parental authority is the foundation of all authority within human society. This means that every opportunity to honor an earthly authority is an opportunity to honor God. In this obedience, God desires to provide us with peace, provision, and protection.

Therefore whoever resists the authorities resists what God has appointed, and those who resist will incur judgment. **(ROMANS 13:2)**

"YOU ARE TO HONOR AND OBEY YOUR FATHER, MOTHER, EV'RY DAY, SERVE THEM EACH WAY THAT COMES TO HAND; YOU'LL THEN LIVE LONG IN THE LAND." **(*LSB* 581:5)**

How can you work to bring peace and harmony to your neighbors?

THE FIFTH COMMANDMENT

YOU SHALL NOT MURDER.

What does this mean? We should fear and love God so that we do not hurt or harm our neighbor in his body, but help and support him in every physical need.

. . . .

Our relationships begin with God, flow through our family, and proceed out from our home into the neighborhood in which we live. We are called to cultivate neighborhoods of peace. Living in harmony with our neighbors and promoting communal well-being helps to fulfill God's plan for human community. All harm, including murder, is forbidden by God and destroys the fabric of community God created. Treating our neighbors in the same way we desire to be treated builds up our neighbors and fulfills God's command.

The Fifth Commandment teaches us how to live with our neighbors. Whereas civil authorities are given the power to correct and punish, individuals are given the unique responsibility of cultivating relationships of neighborly love. While it might seem obvious that we are not to harm our neighbors, this commandment further calls us to protect our neighbors from violence and misfortune and to serve them with a gentle and patient heart. This commandment is an opportunity to practice works of love toward our neighbors even when they would be considered our enemies by the standards of the world.

You shall love the Lord your God with all your heart and with all your soul and with all your strength and with all your mind, and your neighbor as yourself. **(LUKE 10:27)**

LET IT BE OUR CHIEF ENDEAVOR THAT WE MAY THE LORD OBEY, THEN SHALL ENVY CEASE FOREVER AND ALL HATE BE DONE AWAY. *(ELH 421:5)*

What insights about marriage do Jesus' actions and attitudes toward the Church reveal?

THE SIXTH COMMANDMENT

YOU SHALL NOT COMMIT ADULTERY.

What does this mean? We should fear and love God so that we lead a sexually pure and decent life in what we say and do, and husband and wife love and honor each other.

∙ ∙

Of all the earthly estates, God established marriage as the highest. While marriage is a civil arrangement, for Christians, marriage is also an opportunity to model the loving relationship between Christ and His Bride, the Church. The husband's love for his wife is a model of Jesus' self-sacrificial love for His Church and the wife's respect for her husband is a model of the Church's respect for Jesus. Through marriage, the husband and wife enter into a lifelong commitment to mutual submission in reverence to Jesus Christ and, if blessed, the nurturing of children in a safe and loving environment.

In order to strengthen and preserve the marriage bond, fidelity and chastity are essential. The Sixth Commandment teaches us the importance of fidelity within the estate of marriage and chastity in our daily lives. This commandment serves as a hedge around every married couple, protecting their marriage from those who would break its sacred bond. Fidelity and chastity honor the estate of marriage and protect each spouse from disgrace and dishonor. Fidelity and chastity are two of the greatest expressions of love that a spouse can give to the other.

For you were called to freedom, brothers. Only do not use your freedom as an opportunity for the flesh, but through love serve one another.

(GALATIANS 5:13)

NOW GIVE YOUR PRESENCE FROM ABOVE THAT THESE, BY VOWING TRUE, MAY SHOW THEIR PLEDGE IS LIKE THE LOVE BETWEEN THE CHURCH AND YOU. **(*LSB* 859:2)**

How might you preserve your neighbors' property and promote their advantage?

THE SEVENTH COMMANDMENT

YOU SHALL NOT STEAL.

What does this mean? We should fear and love God so that we do not take our neighbor's money or possessions, or get them in any dishonest way, but help him to improve and protect his possessions and income.

. . . .

Stealing our neighbor's property and destroying his livelihood dishonors our neighbor and denies him God's gracious gifts. Theft comes in many forms, including dishonesty, laziness, and malice. Our technological age has made theft easier and easier; it is now commonplace for thieves to use the Internet, social media, and email to steal someone's identity or wealth. But regardless of the means, theft is always displeasing to God and diminishes our neighbor.

The Seventh Commandment teaches us that just as we are to protect our neighbors and their families, so, too, we are to protect their possessions and work to better their lives. Stealing from our neighbors not only takes from them the gifts God has given, but it also is an expression of discontentment with what we have received from God. This commandment calls us to preserve our neighbors' property and provide for our neighbors in time of need. This commandment offers a lifetime of potential good works and charity. By helping our neighbors to succeed and prosper, we better our neighbors, their families, and the community in which our neighbors live.

Let the thief no longer steal, but rather let him labor, doing honest work with his own hands, so that he may have something to share with anyone in need. **(EPHESIANS 4:28)**

WITHHOLD NOT YOUR NEIGHBORS' GOODS. PROTECT THEM AS YOUR OWN.

GIVING PRAISE FOR ALL THEY HAVE, REFLECT THE GRACE YOU'RE SHOWN. **(T. COOK)**

How might you speak well of your neighbors and protect their reputation?

THE EIGHTH COMMANDMENT

YOU SHALL NOT GIVE FALSE TESTIMONY AGAINST YOUR NEIGHBOR.

What does this mean? We should fear and love God so that we do not tell lies about our neighbor, betray him, slander him, or hurt his reputation, but defend him, speak well of him, and explain everything in the kindest way.

. . . .

The most powerful tool for both good and evil is the human tongue. Our tongue can be used to protect the rights and reputation of our neighbors, assist them with their struggle against sin, and put the best construction on their actions and words. But our tongue can also be used to slander our neighbors, diminish their standing in the community, and falsely judge them in the public square. Just as we are commanded to not steal our neighbors' possessions, so, too, we are commanded to not steal our neighbors' honor and reputation by diminishing them with our words.

The Eighth Commandment teaches us that unless we are appointed judge over our neighbors, we are not to pass sentence on their words or deeds. Instead, we are to use our words to assist and support our neighbors in their daily lives. This commandment is fulfilled when we speak well of our neighbors, lovingly work for their reformation, and protect them from dishonor and false witness. When times of conflict and sin arise, we are instructed by Jesus to privately seek reconciliation. If our attempts fail, we are instructed to turn to the Christian community to assist in the restoration of our neighbors and reconcile our relationship with them.

Let no corrupting talk come out of your mouths, but only such as is good for building up, as fits the occasion, that it may give grace to those who hear. **(EPHESIANS 4:29)**

GUARD OUR SPEECH, O LORD WE PRAY, OUR NEIGHBOR TO DEFEND.

WORDS OF GRACE, OUR TONGUES PROCLAIM, THE BOND OF PEACE OUR END. **(T. COOK)**

What good treasure has God placed in the treasury of your heart?

YOU SHALL NOT COVET YOUR NEIGHBOR'S HOUSE.

What does this mean? We should fear and love God so that we do not scheme to get our neighbor's inheritance or house, or get it in a way which only appears right, but help and be of service to him in keeping it.

YOU SHALL NOT COVET YOUR NEIGHBOR'S WIFE, OR HIS MANSERVANT OR MAIDSERVANT, HIS OX OR DONKEY, OR ANYTHING THAT BELONGS TO YOUR NEIGHBOR.

What does this mean? We should fear and love God so that we do not entice or force away our neighbor's wife, workers, or animals, or turn them against him, but urge them to stay and do their duty.

Jesus taught that what a person says and does reflects the kind of treasure stored within the person's heart. A good person produces good things from the treasury of the heart and an evil person produces evil things. Everything that we say and do flows from our heart. In order to change our actions, our heart must be changed as well. The prayer of every Christian is that God will change and renew our heart so that words of grace and works of love might flow forth for the benefit of our neighbors and the glory of God.

The Ninth and Tenth Commandments teach us that not only are the actual acts prohibited in the previous commandments displeasing to God, but so also are the motivations of the heart that provoke them. Jealousy, covetousness, and lack of contentment are all motivating factors behind our desire to take from our neighbors what God has given. While the transgressions revealed in the previous commandments are obvious in nature, the devious attempts to take from our neighbors described in the last two commandments are often hidden under the appearance of honesty and righteousness. The subtle attempts to take our neighbors' possessions through enticement or deceit is forbidden, and instead, a pure heart that seeks to advance and preserve our neighbors is commanded.

Keep your heart with all vigilance, for from it flow the springs of life.

(PROVERBS 4:23)

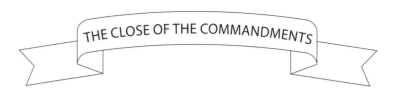

What new insights did you gain from reflecting on the Ten Commandments?

TO THOSE WHO HELP IN CHRIST HAVE FOUND AND WOULD IN WORKS OF LOVE ABOUND

What does God say about all these commandments?

HE SAYS, "I, THE LORD YOUR GOD, AM A JEALOUS GOD, PUNISHING THE CHILDREN FOR THE SIN OF THE FATHERS TO THE THIRD AND FOURTH GENERATION OF THOSE WHO HATE ME, BUT SHOWING LOVE TO A THOUSAND GENERATIONS OF THOSE WHO LOVE ME AND KEEP MY COMMANDMENTS." **(EX. 20:5-6)**

What does this mean? God threatens to punish all who break these commandments. Therefore, we should fear His wrath and not do anything against them. But He promises grace and every blessing to all who keep these commandments. Therefore, we should also love and trust in Him and gladly do what He commands.

· ·

All of God's commandments flow from the First Commandment. By striving to follow the other commandments, we are also fulfilling the first: you shall have no other gods. The promises connected to the Ten Commandments illustrate God's deep desire to see His creation flourish. Honor, respect, and love for God and His creation underscore all that God commands. While many focus on the punishments connected with each command, Luther helps us realize that God's goal is not to punish us, but to fulfill the promises that are attached to each commandment. The Ten Commandments are worthy of our meditation, memory, and practice.

The Close of the Ten Commandments teaches us that God desires to bless those who keep His commandments. His commandments are kept when we express our faith though love for God and our neighbor. The commandments illustrate the two relationships common to all people. The vertical relationship that we have with God is described in the first three commandments, and the horizontal relationship we have with our neighbors is described in the last seven. In striving to fulfill God's commandments, our relationship with Him is strengthened and our neighbors are provided for in a manner that is pleasing to our Creator.

Have nothing to do with irreverent, silly myths. Rather train yourself for godliness; for while bodily training is of some value, godliness is of value in every way, as it holds promise for the present life and also for the life to come. **(1 TIMOTHY 4:7-8)**

IT SHOWS WHAT DEEDS ARE HIS DELIGHT AND SHOULD BE DONE AS GOOD AND RIGHT. *(ELH 492:3)*

THE CREED

THE FIRST ARTICLE: CREATION

I believe in God, the Father Almighty, Maker of heaven and earth.

What does this mean? I believe that God has made me and all creatures; that He has given me my body and soul, eyes, ears, and all my members, my reason and all my senses, and still takes care of them.

He also gives me clothing and shoes, food and drink, house and home, wife and children, land, animals, and all I have. He richly and daily provides me with all that I need to support this body and life.

He defends me against all danger and guards and protects me from all evil.

All this He does only out of fatherly, divine goodness and mercy, without any merit or worthiness in me. For all this it is my duty to thank and praise, serve and obey Him.

This is most certainly true.

While the Ten Commandments describe God's will and His promises, the Apostles' Creed describes God. God the Father is a creative God. God's creative work is seen in the beauty and intricacy of the world around us. The changing of the seasons, the migration of birds, the fingerprints of a newborn child are all brushstrokes of His creative work. Like an expert artist, God speaks onto the blank canvas of the universe a masterpiece that is uniquely His. Everything that exists, including ourselves, is God's workmanship.

The First Article teaches us that God is the Great Provider. Everything that exists is a creative expression of His divine love and goodness. Creation was brought into existence and continues to be maintained by the triune God. The continual creative activity of God is not based on our merit or worthiness, but on our Creator's kindness and grace. To acknowledge that God is our Creator is to confess that we, along with all living things, are His creatures. As creatures who live before God in His creation, we seek to serve Him by being faithful stewards of what He has made.

What parts of God's creation are you most thankful for?

For every house is built by someone, but the builder of all things is God. **(HEBREWS 3:4)**

HE HAS DONE MARVELOUS THINGS.

I TOO WILL PRAISE HIM WITH A NEW SONG! *(LSB 817:REFRAIN)*

What does Jesus' humiliation teach you about God's love?

And in Jesus Christ, His only Son, our Lord, who was conceived by the Holy Spirit, born of the Virgin Mary, suffered under Pontius Pilate, was crucified, died and was buried. He descended into hell. The third day He rose again from the dead. He ascended into heaven and sits at the right hand of God, the Father Almighty. From thence He will come to judge the living and the dead.

What does this mean? I believe that Jesus Christ, true God, begotten of the Father from eternity, and also true man, born of the Virgin Mary, is my Lord, who has redeemed me, a lost and condemned person, purchased and won me from all sins, from death, and from the power of the devil; not with gold or silver, but with His holy, precious blood and with His innocent suffering and death, that I may be His own and live under Him in His kingdom and serve Him in everlasting righteousness, innocence, and blessedness, just as He is risen from the dead, lives and reigns to all eternity.

This is most certainly true.

Humanity's rebellion against God broke the relationship between the Creator and His creatures. Like a damaged work of art, creation was no longer as God designed or intended. The creative work of God had been marred with sin, but God did not give up on what He had made. He determined to restore His magnificent work. God entered His creation in order to restore His masterpiece from the inside out.

The Second Article teaches us that in Jesus, God became part of His creation in order to restore and reconcile the creation to Himself. Jesus began His work of redeeming the world by humbling Himself. This process of humility began with Jesus' incarnation, continued through His ministry, and resulted in His willingness to be crucified and die so all of creation might be reconciled to His Father. The personal union between God and man in Jesus is one of the greatest mysteries of the Christian faith. In Jesus' humiliation, the creation that was separated from God because of humanity's rebellion is forgiven, and the relationship between creation and Creator is restored.

And being found in human form, He humbled Himself by becoming obedient to the point of death, even death on a cross.

(PHILIPPIANS 2:8)

THE SECOND ARTICLE: REDEMPTION—JESUS' EXALTATION

What does Jesus' exaltation mean for your faith?

And in Jesus Christ, His only Son, our Lord, who was conceived by the Holy Spirit, born of the Virgin Mary, suffered under Pontius Pilate, was crucified, died and was buried. He descended into hell. The third day He rose again from the dead. He ascended into heaven and sits at the right hand of God, the Father Almighty. From thence He will come to judge the living and the dead.

What does this mean? I believe that Jesus Christ, true God, begotten of the Father from eternity, and also true man, born of the Virgin Mary, is my Lord, who has redeemed me, a lost and condemned person, purchased and won me from all sins, from death, and from the power of the devil; not with gold or silver, but with His holy, precious blood and with His innocent suffering and death, that I may be His own and live under Him in His kingdom and serve Him in everlasting righteousness, innocence, and blessedness, just as He is risen from the dead, lives and reigns to all eternity.

This is most certainly true.

In Jesus' death, the work of reconciliation was complete. The peace between God and humanity proclaimed by the angels at Jesus' birth was accomplished. The relationship between the Creator and His creation was restored. Now that Jesus had fulfilled His mission, it was time for Him to emerge from His period of humiliation and share His victory with the world. The depth of Jesus' humiliation gave way to the height of His exaltation.

The Second Article teaches us that once Jesus' work of redemption was complete, He announced His victory over sin, death, and the devil to those who had died before Him. This announcement signaled that His time of humiliation had come to an end. Upon His resurrection, His victory was proclaimed to His followers. Before His ascension into heaven, Jesus commissioned His followers to take the announcement of His victory to the world. He promised to assist them in their mission by sending the Holy Spirit.

God has highly exalted Him and bestowed on Him the name that is above every name, so that at the name of Jesus every knee should bow, in heaven and on earth and under the earth, and every tongue confess that Jesus Christ is Lord, to the glory of God the Father.

(PHILIPPIANS 2:9–11)

What do you look forward to when Jesus returns?

And in Jesus Christ, His only Son, our Lord, who was conceived by the Holy Spirit, born of the Virgin Mary, suffered under Pontius Pilate, was crucified, died and was buried. He descended into hell. The third day He rose again from the dead. He ascended into heaven and sits at the right hand of God, the Father Almighty. From thence He will come to judge the living and the dead.

What does this mean? I believe that Jesus Christ, true God, begotten of the Father from eternity, and also true man, born of the Virgin Mary, is my Lord, who has redeemed me, a lost and condemned person, purchased and won me from all sins, from death, and from the power of the devil; not with gold or silver, but with His holy, precious blood and with His innocent suffering and death, that I may be His own and live under Him in His kingdom and serve Him in everlasting righteousness, innocence, and blessedness, just as He is risen from the dead, lives and reigns to all eternity.

This is most certainly true.

Jesus' ascension signals a time of preparation and proclamation. As we await Jesus' return, we prepare ourselves for the new world to come—living in eager expectation and dedicating ourselves to sharing the message of salvation with the world. We train our eyes toward heaven, knowing that when His preparations are complete, we will see Jesus face-to-face. For those who oppose Jesus and His message of salvation, Jesus' return will be one of judgment; but for all those who trust in Jesus for salvation, His return will be a celebration of His saving grace and unending love.

The Second Article teaches us that upon Jesus' return, He will separate us from sin, death, and the forces of the devil that continue to be present with us today. This final separation of God's children from all those who would oppose Jesus and His kingdom will usher in the completion of Jesus' work of restoration. Jesus, who came in humility, will return as Lord of all and His righteous reign will be revealed. The creation that bears the marks of sin will pass away and the new creation will emerge. On that day, God will restore all of creation, including us. In our new bodies, we will live in God's new creation under the never-ending reign of Jesus.

And then they will see the Son of Man coming in a cloud with power and great glory. **(LUKE 21:27)**

FROM OUR FEARS AND SINS RELEASE US; LET US FIND OUR REST IN THEE. *(LSB 338:1)*

THE THIRD ARTICLE: SANCTIFICATION

Where do you see the Holy Spirit at work today?

I believe in the Holy Spirit, the holy Christian church, the communion of saints, the forgiveness of sins, the resurrection of the body, and the life everlasting. Amen.

What does this mean? I believe that I cannot by my own reason or strength believe in Jesus Christ, my Lord, or come to Him; but the Holy Spirit has called me by the Gospel, enlightened me with His gifts, sanctified and kept me in the true faith.

In the same way He calls, gathers, enlightens, and sanctifies the whole Christian church on earth, and keeps it with Jesus Christ in the one true faith.

In this Christian church He daily and richly forgives all my sins and the sins of all believers.

On the Last Day He will raise me and all the dead, and give eternal life to me and all believers in Christ.

This is most certainly true.

As we await Jesus' return, we are not left alone. God the Father and the Son have sent the Holy Spirit to establish His Church. Working through the Word and the Sacraments, the Holy Spirit is preparing His people, making us holy. While the word *church* is used in various ways, the true Church is the people of God who gather together around Word and Sacrament. Through God's Word in its various forms, the Holy Spirit creates and strengthens the faith of all Christians, preparing us for Jesus' return.

The Third Article teaches us that the Holy Spirit, working through the Word of God, builds God's community—the Church. Within this Church, grace is proclaimed, faith is created, and our hearts are opened so we might understand our need for Jesus and the salvation that He has won. Without the Holy Spirit working through the Gospel of Jesus Christ, we would be lost and the message of Jesus would not be proclaimed. It is through God the Holy Spirit that Jesus' commission is fulfilled and people are brought to faith.

But you were washed, you were sanctified, you were justified in the name of the Lord Jesus Christ and by the Spirit of our God.

(1 CORINTHIANS 6:11B)

O SOURCE OF UNCREATED LIGHT, THE BEARER OF GOD'S GRACIOUS MIGHT. THRICE-HOLY FOUNT,

THRICE-HOLY FIRE, OUR HEARTS WITH HEAV'NLY LOVE INSPIRE. **(LSB 500:2)**

How does God's invitation to call Him Father impact your Christian life?

THE INTRODUCTION

OUR FATHER WHO ART IN HEAVEN.

What does this mean? With these words God tenderly invites us to believe that He is our true Father and that we are His true children, so that with all boldness and confidence we may ask Him as dear children ask their dear father.

. . . .

How do we relate to an all-knowing, all-seeing, and all-powerful God? While we know who God is, what He does, and what He wills for our life, we also need to know how to address Him. The thought of approaching the great I AM who created all things can be intimidating. Jesus' instruction to pray to His Father as our Father provides us with a beautiful way to approach God in prayer. The opening salutation of the Lord's Prayer removes our uncertainty and hesitancy in addressing God by reminding us of our identity as His children.

The Introduction to the Lord's Prayer teaches us that because of Jesus, we are free to approach God in the same way that a child approaches a loving Father. To call upon God as our Father is the essence of prayer and is a fulfillment of the First and Second Commandments. Prayer is not left to our desires; it is a command of God and a confirmation that we acknowledge Him as the source of all good things. Because it is the will of the Father that we call upon His name in prayer, we have the assurance that He hears us and will provide what we need.

But now that faith has come, we are no longer under a guardian, for in Christ Jesus you are all sons of God, through faith. **(GALATIANS 3:25–26)**

What have your actions and words of this last week said about your Father?

HALLOWED BE THY NAME.

What does this mean? God's name is certainly holy in itself, but we pray in this petition that it may be kept holy among us also.

How is God's name kept holy? God's name is kept holy when the Word of God is taught in its truth and purity, and we, as the children of God, also lead holy lives according to it. Help us to do this, dear Father in heaven! But anyone who teaches or lives contrary to God's Word profanes the name of God among us. Protect us from this, heavenly Father!

. . . .

The actions of children reflect on their parents. When we act in a dishonorable way, we dishonor our parents, our siblings, and our family as a whole. As Christians, we are called to live in a way that reflects well on our Father. Our actions, words, and witness are to reflect our connection and relationship to God. This petition is an expression of our commitment to fulfill the Second Commandment and a request to God that He would assist us in fulfilling it. To pray that God's name is kept holy is to pray that our words and deeds would give Him honor and praise.

The First Petition of the Lord's Prayer teaches us that God's name is holy, and we are to use God's name in holy ways. The holy use of God's name is a result of our connection with Him. As His children, all that we have and do is connected to God. Using God's name in holy ways keeps His name holy in our daily lives, just as it is in heaven. Through our adoption as children of God through the saving work of Jesus, we have become representatives of our Father in the world and everything we do is a reflection of Him to those around us.

Bless the LORD, O my soul, and all that is within me, bless His holy name! **(PSALM 103:1)**

YOUR NAME BE HALLOWED. HELP US, LORD, IN PURITY TO KEEP YOUR WORD,

THAT TO THE GLORY OF YOUR NAME WE WALK BEFORE YOU FREE FROM BLAME. *(LSB 766:2)*

How does the security and blessing of God's kingdom impact your daily life?

THY KINGDOM COME.

What does this mean? The kingdom of God certainly comes by itself without our prayer, but we pray in this petition that it may come to us also.

How does God's kingdom come? God's kingdom comes when our heavenly Father gives us His Holy Spirit, so that by His grace we believe His holy Word and lead godly lives here in time and there in eternity.

• •

The kingdom of God comes in ways that we might not expect. While many picture the coming of God's kingdom when Jesus returns, Jesus explains that the kingdom of God is already in our midst. It is our prayer that we might enter God's kingdom and be recipients of the gracious gifts it contains. It might seem presumptuous to request that God's kingdom would come to us and that we might share in its blessings, but God desires to abundantly bless us as members of His kingdom. Jesus confirms this desire by teaching us that when we make it our priority in life to seek the kingdom of God, everything else that we need will be given.

The Second Petition of the Lord's Prayer teaches us to pray that God's kingdom would be present in our lives and that through our lives, others might be brought into God's kingdom of grace as well. This petition is an expression of our confidence in God's provision and our willingness to live in His kingdom and under His reign. It is also a request that others might be added to His kingdom through the working of the Holy Spirit.

The time is fulfilled, and the kingdom of God is at hand, repent and believe in the gospel.

(MARK 1:15)

How has God strengthened you to follow and promote His will?

YOUR GRACIOUS WILL ON EARTH BE DONE AS IT IS DONE BEFORE YOUR THRONE, . . .

THE THIRD PETITION

THY WILL BE DONE ON EARTH AS IT IS IN HEAVEN.

What does this mean? The good and gracious will of God is done even without our prayer, but we pray in this petition that it may be done among us also.

How is God's will done? God's will is done when He breaks and hinders every evil plan and purpose of the devil, the world, and our sinful nature, which do not want us to hallow God's name or let His kingdom come; and when He strengthens and keeps us firm in His Word and faith until we die. This is His good and gracious will.

• •

Submission to the will of God is the rejection of our own will. To put the will of God first, even when it means that we will experience suffering, is clearly modeled for us in the life of Jesus. When facing His pending arrest, abuse, and ultimate death, Jesus prayed in the garden that His Father's will would be fulfilled. This willing submission to the will of God is a prayer not only for ourselves, but also for the world. When the enemies of God and His Word seek their will over His, they become a hindrance to the proclamation of the Gospel.

The Third Petition of the Lord's Prayer teaches us the importance of praying for God's will to be done as opposed to the will of those who would resist God and His Word. This petition is a prayer of willing obedience and a request for protection from the evil motivations found in the world and even in ourselves. As members of God's kingdom, we work to remove any obstacle that inhibits God's will, even if it means that we ourselves suffer as a result. For we know that our suffering, like that of Jesus, is not in vain.

For this is the will of My Father, that every-one who looks on the Son and believes in Him should have eternal life, and I will raise Him up on the last day. **(JOHN 6:40)**

CURB FLESH AND BLOOD AND EV'RY ILL THAT SETS ITSELF AGAINST YOUR WILL. **(LSB 766:4)**

What kind of "daily bread" does your family and community need most today?

SAVE US FROM HARDSHIP, WAR, AND STRIFE; IN PLAGUE AND FAMINE, SPARE OUR LIFE,

THE FOURTH PETITION

GIVE US THIS DAY OUR DAILY BREAD.

What does this mean? God certainly gives daily bread to everyone without our prayers, even to all evil people, but we pray in this petition that God would lead us to realize this and to receive our daily bread with thanksgiving.

What is meant by daily bread? Daily bread includes everything that has to do with the support and needs of the body, such as food, drink, clothing, shoes, house, home, land, animals, money, goods, a devout husband or wife, devout children, devout workers, devout and faithful rulers, good government, good weather, peace, health, self-control, good reputation, good friends, faithful neighbors, and the like.

· ·

As we seek to fulfill God's will and work toward the expansion of His kingdom, we need God's help in fulfilling our daily needs. As His creatures, our physical and relational health is vital to our human endeavors. In order to dedicate ourselves fully to the work of the kingdom, God invites us to request from Him everything necessary. God answers our request by providing for and maintaining all of creation. Not only does God provide food and clothes, but He also provides the ecosystem, weather, health, and populations necessary to make and deliver the world's daily necessities.

The Fourth Petition of the Lord's Prayer teaches us to pray for all the needs of our earthly life, the means through which God delivers them, and the protection from anything that would frustrate His gracious provision. Along with this provision, we also pray for peace and harmony within the homes and communities throughout the world so that God's gifts might be enjoyed and administered properly. This includes the request for a stable government and faithful leaders that work for peace, security, and happiness throughout the world, as well as the rejection of greed and the gift of a thankful heart.

But seek first the kingdom of God and His righteousness, and all these things will be added to you. **(MATTHEW 6:33)**

THAT WE IN HONEST PEACE MAY LIVE, TO CARE AND GREED NO ENTRANCE GIVE. *(LSB 766:5)*

What areas of your life need the light of God's forgiveness?

AND FORGIVE US OUR TRESPASSES AS WE FORGIVE THOSE WHO TRESPASS AGAINST US.

What does this mean? We pray in this petition that our Father in heaven would not look at our sins, or deny our prayer because of them. We are neither worthy of the things for which we pray, nor have we deserved them, but we ask that He would give them all to us by grace, for we daily sin much and surely deserve nothing but punishment. So we too will sincerely forgive and gladly do good to those who sin against us.

. . . .

While we were still enemies of God, God sent His Son, Jesus Christ, to atone for the sins of the world. The motivation for this gracious act is not found in our worthiness or even our request. God's forgiveness is a result of His love for His creation. God's love for the world set into motion the plan of salvation that was completed in the death and resurrection of Jesus. While God's forgiveness is abundant and given to all, there are many who are unaware of His grace or continue to live as enemies of God. God desires everyone to turn toward Him, repent of their sin, and live a life of freedom in the Gospel of His Son—a life that reflects the forgiveness they have received.

The Fifth Petition of the Lord's Prayer teaches us that while the forgiveness Jesus won for us is given without our prayer, we are to pray that we would recognize this forgiveness and forgive others as we have been forgiven. This petition is also an acknowledgment that even though we are God's children, we still sin. Our continued sin reminds us that without God's grace in Jesus, we would be lost. As we struggle against our sinful inclinations, God reminds us of His forgiving love through His Word and Sacraments.

But the tax collector, standing far off, would not even lift up his eyes to heaven, but beat his breast, saying, "God, be merciful to me, a sinner!" **(LUKE 18:13)**

FORGIVE OUR SINS, LORD, WE IMPLORE, THAT THEY MAY TROUBLE US NO MORE; . . .

HELP US IN OUR COMMUNITY TO SERVE EACH OTHER WILLINGLY. **(LSB 766:6)**

SO WE TOO
WILL SINCERELY
FORGIVE AND
GLADLY DO GOOD
TO THOSE WHO
SIN AGAINST US.

From what attacks do you need God to protect you?

WHERE OUR GRIM FOE AND ALL HIS HORDE WOULD VEX OUR SOULS ON EV'RY HAND. HELP US RESIST,

AND LEAD US NOT INTO TEMPTATION.

What does this mean? God tempts no one. We pray in this petition that God would guard and keep us so that the devil, the world, and our sinful nature may not deceive us or mislead us into false belief, despair, and other great shame and vice. Although we are attacked by these things, we pray that we may finally overcome them and win the victory.

· ·

Our faith and life are under constant assault. The struggle against temptation is a daily battle. We are frequently tempted by the devil, the world, and our own sinful inclinations to stray from God and fall into disbelief and despair. Without God's constant protection from these opposing forces and provision of strength through His Word and Sacraments, we would lose the battle. While there are days when it seems the whole world is working against us, God is always working for us, assuring us of the victory that has been won by Jesus.

The Sixth Petition of the Lord's Prayer teaches us to pray to God for protection and strength. As long as we live in this fallen world, we will be assaulted with temptations and encouraged to reject our faith. This prayer is a heartfelt plea to God to help us resist those temptations, just as Jesus resisted the temptations of the devil in His earthly ministry. God has promised to be our refuge and strength in times of temptation, arming us with His Word to fight. While temptations are always present, attacking us from without and from within, God reminds us that in Jesus, the battle is already won and victory is ours.

Let no one say when he is tempted, "I am being tempted by God," for God cannot be tempted with evil, and He Himself tempts no one. But each person is tempted when he is lured and enticed by his own desire.

(JAMES 1:13–14)

How has God protected you from the devil and his schemes?

BUT DELIVER US FROM EVIL.

What does this mean? We pray in this petition, in summary, that our Father in heaven would rescue us from every evil of body and soul, possessions and reputation, and finally, when our last hour comes, give us a blessed end, and graciously take us from this valley of sorrow to Himself in heaven.

· ·

The devil's prayer is that our prayers to God would not be answered. He desires God to be dishonored, God's children to be overcome by sin, and ultimately to scatter the sheep of Jesus' fold. The devil's desires are the exact opposite of everything that Jesus has taught us to pray in this prayer. The devil desires the destruction of God's kingdom and the establishment of his own—a kingdom not of love and mercy, but of misery and death. With the exception of Jesus, no human can fully resist him. This is why we pray for God's protection and the devil's defeat.

The Seventh Petition of the Lord's Prayer teaches us to offer our prayers in direct opposition to the devil himself, the father of all lies and the source of human misery. Everything we do as children of God is done to interfere with the devil's plans and in faithfulness to God. While ultimately overcome by Jesus' death and resurrection, the devil still seeks to undo God's creative and gracious work. This final petition is a clear declaration of our rejection of the devil and his schemes. It declares that God is our Lord and makes known our desire for everything that opposes Him to be overcome until we are finally home with our Lord.

But the Lord is faithful. He will establish you and guard you against the evil one.

(2 THESSALONIANS 3:3)

REDEEM US FROM ETERNAL DEATH, AND, WHEN WE YIELD OUR DYING BREATH,

CONSOLE US, GRANT US CALM RELEASE, AND TAKE OUR SOULS TO YOU IN PEACE. *(LSB 766:8)*

How does what you believe about the nature of God impact your confidence in prayer?

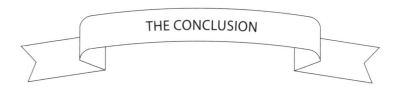

THE CONCLUSION

FOR THINE IS THE KINGDOM AND THE POWER AND THE GLORY FOREVER AND EVER. AMEN.

What does this mean? This means that I should be certain that these petitions are pleasing to our Father in heaven, and are heard by Him; for He Himself has commanded us to pray in this way and has promised to hear us. Amen, amen means "yes, yes, it shall be so."

· ·

The Lord's Prayer begins and concludes with our confession about the identity of God. God is the almighty Father to whom all glory is given and to whom all requests are directed. As we close our prayer, we affirm the relationship between Creator and creature. All things belong to God and it is through Him and Him alone that we receive the good things we need. The prayer that Jesus gave is not only a command, but also a privilege. To come before God in this intimate way as His children is a direct result of the reconciliation won for us by Jesus. Because of Jesus, we are no longer enemies of God, but His children.

The Conclusion to the Lord's Prayer teaches us that the entire prayer Jesus taught is directed to a God who not only encourages and hears the prayers we offer, but also has the power to fulfill our prayers. The Conclusion serves as a capstone and an affirmation. It is our acknowledgment that God alone is in control and that all we say and do is done in recognition of who God is and what He does in our lives. To God and God alone belongs the kingdom, the power, and the glory. The prayer concludes with our amen—a statement confirming our desire that God's will be done in our lives and in the world.

To the King of the ages, immortal, invisible, the only God, be honor and glory forever and ever, Amen. **(1 TIMOTHY 1:17)**

AMEN, THAT IS, SO SHALL IT BE. MAKE STRONG OUR FAITH IN YOU,

THAT WE MAY DOUBT NOT BUT WITH TRUST BELIEVE THAT WHAT WE ASK WE SHALL RECEIVE. *(LSB 766:9)*

THE SACRAMENT OF HOLY BAPTISM

THE SACRAMENT OF HOLY BAPTISM (PART ONE)

How does your Baptism give you certainty in your identity as a child of God?

What is Baptism? Baptism is not just plain water, but it is the water included in God's command and combined with God's word.

Which is that word of God? Christ our Lord says in the last chapter of Matthew: "Therefore go and make disciples of all nations, baptizing them in the name of the Father and of the Son and of the Holy Spirit." (Matt. 28:19)

• •

Baptism is one of the two activities commanded by Jesus in His commission to make disciples. Baptism is both the entry into new life and the beginning of our struggle to live that new life faithfully before God. When questioned by Nicodemus regarding how one might be born into God's kingdom, Jesus points to Baptism as the way to new life and rebirth. Baptism is not merely a required ritual; it is the powerful combination of water and God's Word that produces new life and membership in God's Kingdom for all who believe.

The catechism teaches us that Baptism is commanded by God and not created by humans. It is more than a symbolic act that signifies our new life in Christ. To be baptized in the name of the triune God is to be baptized by God Himself. Baptism is God working through His Word to connect those who are baptized to the life, death, and resurrection of Jesus. The new life given in Baptism is the life of Christ. Without God's Word, Baptism is nothing more than water, but with God's Word, it becomes a sacred act, a Sacrament commanded and fulfilled by God.

Having been buried with Him in baptism, in which you were also raised with Him through faith in the powerful working of God, who raised Him from the dead. **(COLOSSIANS 2:12)**

MY LOVING FATHER, HERE YOU TAKE ME TO BE HENCEFORTH YOUR CHILD AND HEIR.

IN THE NAME OF THE FATHER AND
OF THE SON AND OF THE HOLY SPIRIT.

THE SACRAMENT OF HOLY BAPTISM (PART TWO)

How can you use the gift of new life that you have received from God to glorify Him?

What benefits does Baptism give? It works forgiveness of sins, rescues from death and the devil, and gives eternal salvation to all who believe this, as the words and promises of God declare.

Which are these words and promises of God? Christ our Lord says in the last chapter of Mark: "Whoever believes and is baptized will be saved, but whoever does not believe will be condemned." (Mark 16:16)

. . . .

Throughout our lives, we receive many gifts. Some gifts celebrate special events, others are tokens of thanks and appreciation; what all gifts have in common, though, is that they are given. Yet the giving of a gift is only part of the equation. In order for a person to benefit from what the gift contains, the gift must be received. It is through the reception of the gift that the intent of the giver is fulfilled. To reject a gift is to dishonor the giver and miss the benefit the gift contains. In Baptism, God gives the gift of new life in Christ. Through faith, the gift of new life is received.

The catechism teaches us that the purpose of Baptism is to give the gift of salvation. Through Baptism, we are delivered from sin, death, and the devil and are made members of the kingdom of God. Those who receive Baptism in faith by believing in Jesus, who made it possible, find within this gift an incomparable treasure. Baptism, and the gracious gift of salvation that it contains, is a vivid reminder that our salvation is not the result of our own work or merit but is freely given by God. There is no need to earn what is given for free.

For in Christ Jesus you are all sons of God, through faith. For as many of you as were baptized into Christ have put on Christ.

(GALATIANS 3:26–27)

ALL WHO BELIEVE AND ARE BAPTIZED SHALL SEE THE LORD'S SALVATION;

BAPTIZED INTO THE DEATH OF CHRIST, THEY ARE A NEW CREATION. *(LSB 601:1)*

THE SACRAMENT OF HOLY BAPTISM (PART THREE)

How does God's generous gift of rebirth in washing and His Word assist you in your daily life?

How can water do such great things? Certainly not just water, but the word of God in and with the water does these things, along with the faith which trusts this word of God in the water. For without God's word the water is plain water and no Baptism. But with the word of God it is a Baptism, that is, a life-giving water, rich in grace, and a washing of the new birth in the Holy Spirit, as St. Paul says in Titus, chapter three: "He saved us through the washing of rebirth and renewal by the Holy Spirit, whom He poured out on us generously through Jesus Christ our Savior, so that, having been justified by His grace, we might become heirs having the hope of eternal life. This is a trustworthy saying." (Titus 3:5–8)

Good things can come in ordinary packages. A letter from a long-forgotten friend can arrive in a plain envelope. A token of love can be enclosed in a box wrapped in newspaper. Many times, a gift's external appearance may cause us to underestimate what is contained inside or even doubt that it contains a gift at all. The mystery of Baptism is that something as simple as water can contain such a powerful gift—the gift of salvation in Jesus.

The catechism teaches us that water alone does not save. While water is useful for many things—such as cleaning our bodies—cleansing us from sin and its effects is beyond water's natural powers. It is only through the mysterious combination of water and the Word of God that Baptism obtains its tremendous power. When combined with God's Word, the waters of Baptism impart the Holy Spirit, and rebirth and renewal occur. When received in faith, those who are baptized take possession of the blessings and benefits of the work of Jesus. The gift of Baptism unites us to Jesus' death, and we emerge connected to His life.

For in one Spirit we were all baptized into one body—Jews or Greeks, slaves or free—and all were made to drink of one Spirit.

(1 CORINTHIANS 12:13)

WE CANNOT SEE THE HOLY THREE CONCEALED THE FONT WITHIN.

MERE WATER SEEMS THE MYSTERY THAT CLEANSES US FROM SIN. *(ELH 245:2)*

THE SACRAMENT OF HOLY BAPTISM (PART FOUR)

How does the certainty of your baptismal identity assist in daily repentance?

What does such baptizing with water indicate? It indicates that the Old Adam in us should by daily contrition and repentance be drowned and die with all sins and evil desires, and that a new man should daily emerge and arise to live before God in righteousness and purity forever.

Where is this written? St. Paul writes in Romans chapter six: "We were therefore buried with Him through baptism into death in order that, just as Christ was raised from the dead through the glory of the Father, we too may live a new life." (Rom. 6:4)

• •

Living our new life faithfully is a constant struggle. Our old habits, sins, and way of thinking still remain even when our new life begins, but fortunately, our Baptism remains as well. Although Baptism only happens once in our life, because it is the work of God, it is a permanent gift. Even when we are unfaithful, God is faithful to His promises found in Baptism. As a result, Baptism, and the new life that it gives, is ours forever. Our daily struggle begins by acknowledging that even though we are children of God, we still sin. The daily process of repentance is the process of changing our mind, heart, and life to be consistent with the new identity we have been given. Our Baptism is the unshakable reminder of who and whose we are as children of God.

The catechism teaches us that the Christian life is one in which the old Adam and new Adam are in conflict. Baptism is an ever-abiding gift that assists us in our struggle. We are not only to be baptized, but we are to walk daily in our new baptismal identity. Through this process, we are assisted by the Holy Spirit and are given the tools of repentance, prayer, and the power of God. These help us in our fight to suppress our sinful ways and work to allow our new selves to emerge.

He saved us, not because of works done by us in righteousness, but according to His own mercy, by the washing of regeneration and renewal of the Holy Spirit. **(TITUS 3:5)**

Which of the Ten Commandments do you struggle the most to keep?

A BROKEN HEART, MY GOD, MY KING! IS ALL THE SACRIFICE I BRING.

CONFESSION

CONFESSION: CONFESS OUR SINS

What is Confession? Confession has two parts. First, that we confess our sins, and second, that we receive absolution, that is, forgiveness, from the pastor as from God Himself, not doubting, but firmly believing that by it our sins are forgiven before God in heaven.

What sins should we confess? Before God we should plead guilty of all sins, even those we are not aware of, as we do in the Lord's Prayer; but before the pastor we should confess only those sins which we know and feel in our hearts.

Which are these? Consider your place in life according to the Ten Commandments: Are you a father, mother, son, daughter, husband, wife, or worker? Have you been disobedient, unfaithful, or lazy? Have you been hot-tempered, rude, or quarrelsome? Have you hurt someone by your words or deeds? Have you stolen, been negligent, wasted anything, or done any harm?

. . . .

When we reflect on the struggle to live our new life in Jesus, we recognize our failures and our need for change. While we are children of God, we are children of God who yet sin. Our failure to faithfully live our daily life would become overwhelming if we did not have a way to share our shortcomings with God and be assured of His forgiveness in Jesus. Confessing our sins and repenting of our failure to live according to God's will enables us to place our sins before God. Through repentance, we can unburden our hearts before a loving and all-forgiving God.

The catechism teaches us that repentance is not done to merit God's grace, nor are our works payment for failures. Repentance is our cry to God to change and renew our life so we might be refreshed in our struggle to live a life worthy of our calling as redeemed children. Repentance is done within our baptismal relationship with God. God is faithful even when we are not, and because of the atoning work of Jesus, we need not fear coming to God with our sins and shortcomings.

If we say we have no sin, we deceive ourselves, and the truth is not in us. If we confess our sins, He is faithful and just to forgive us our sins and to cleanse us from all unrighteousness.

(1 JOHN 1:8-9)

THE GOD OF GRACE WILL NE'ER DESPISE A BROKEN HEART FOR SACRIFICE. **(ISAAC WATTS)**

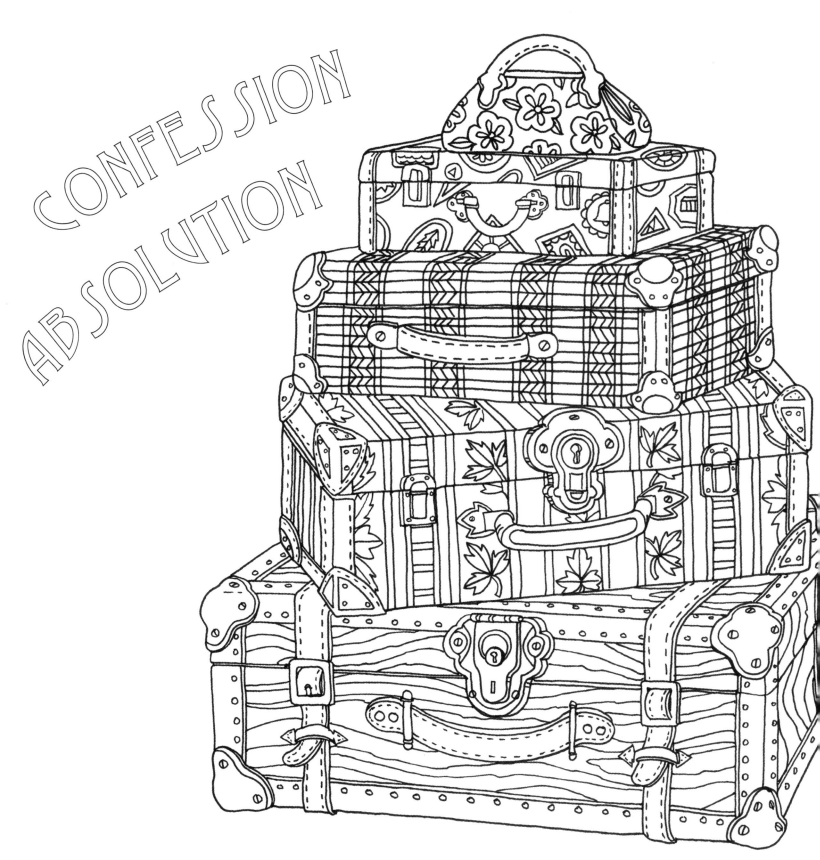

For what sins in your life do you desire to receive absolution?

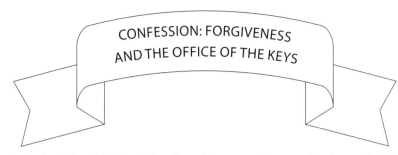

CONFESSION: FORGIVENESS AND THE OFFICE OF THE KEYS

What is the Office of the Keys? The Office of the Keys is that special authority which Christ has given to His church on earth to forgive the sins of repentant sinners, but to withhold forgiveness from the unrepentant as long as they do not repent.

Where is this written? This is what St. John the Evangelist writes in chapter twenty: The Lord Jesus breathed on His disciples and said, "Receive the Holy Spirit. If you forgive anyone his sins, they are forgiven; if you do not forgive them, they are not forgiven." (John 20:22–23)

What do you believe according to these words? I believe that when the called ministers of Christ deal with us by His divine command, in particular when they exclude openly unrepentant sinners from the Christian congregation and absolve those who repent of their sins and want to do better, this is just as valid and certain, even in heaven, as if Christ our dear Lord dealt with us Himself.

. . . .

Just as we desire to hear words of forgiveness from family and friends whom we have hurt, it is also our desire to hear words of forgiveness from God. When words of absolution are spoken, we experience joy and reassurance that our relationship with God remains. In order to rejoice in the assurance of God's forgiveness, Jesus has established the Office of the Keys. The Office of the Keys is the command given by Jesus to withhold the proclamation of forgiveness from those who are unrepentant and to pronounce forgiveness to those who repent.

The catechism teaches us that the Office of the Keys finds its origin in the very words of Jesus to His disciples. Withholding and forgiving sins is the most powerful way for minsters to assist Christians in their daily struggle against sin. The assurance of God's forgiveness in Jesus comes in many forms. Private confession, public confession, the preaching of God's Word, and the reception of the Lord's Supper are all ways in which God works through His ministers to make His forgiveness known.

What I have forgiven …has been for your sake in the presence of Christ. **(2 CORINTHIANS 2:10)**

THE WORDS WHICH ABSOLUTION GIVE ARE HIS WHO DIED THAT WE MIGHT LIVE; THE MINISTER WHOM CHRIST HAS SENT IS BUT HIS HUMBLE INSTRUMENT. **(LSB 614:5)**

What does the certainty of Christ's body and blood in the Sacrament of the Altar mean for you?

CHRIST HIMSELF, THE PRIEST PRESIDING, YET IN BREAD AND WINE ABIDING IN THIS HOLY SACRAMENT,

THE SACRAMENT OF THE ALTAR (PART ONE)

What is the Sacrament of the Altar? It is the true body and blood of our Lord Jesus Christ under the bread and wine, instituted by Christ Himself for us Christians to eat and to drink.

Where is this written? The holy Evangelists Matthew, Mark, Luke, and St. Paul write:

Our Lord Jesus Christ, on the night when He was betrayed, took bread, and when He had given thanks, He broke it and gave it to the disciples and said: "Take, eat; this is My body, which is given for you. This do in remembrance of Me."

In the same way also He took the cup after supper, and when He had given thanks, He gave it to them, saying, "Drink of it, all of you; this cup is the new testament in My blood, which is shed for you for the forgiveness of sins. This do, as often as you drink it, in remembrance of Me."

• •

The Sacrament of the Altar is the work of God given to us through human and earthly means. Because it is God working through the bread and the wine, the Sacrament of the Altar does not depend on the worthiness of the person who gives it or receives it. When we eat the bread and drink the wine, we have assurance that because it is based on God's work and His Word, Christ's body and blood are truly present.

The catechism teaches us that the Sacrament of the Altar, like the Sacrament of Baptism, is commanded by Jesus. It is a personal gift—for each of us—in which the body and blood of Christ are given in, with, and under the bread and the wine. Just as in Baptism, the Word of God and the gift of forgiveness it provides are attached to simple everyday things. By the power of the Word, the bread and the wine convey to each of us Jesus' very body and blood. This meal provides an intimate opportunity to remember the sacrifice of Jesus Christ until He comes again by partaking of the very body and blood that was sacrificed for the forgiveness of our sins.

As often as you eat this bread and drink the cup, you proclaim the Lord's death until He comes. **(1 CORINTHIANS 11:26)**

GIVES THE BREAD OF LIFE, ONCE BROKEN, AND THE CUP, THE PRECIOUS TOKEN OF HIS SACRED COVENANT. *(LSB 620:2)*

How have you been strengthened and refreshed by the Sacrament of the Altar in your daily journey?

THE SACRAMENT OF THE ALTAR (PART TWO)

What is the benefit of this eating and drinking? These words, "Given and shed for you for the forgiveness of sins," show us that in the Sacrament forgiveness of sins, life, and salvation are given us through these words. For where there is forgiveness of sins, there is also life and salvation.

How can bodily eating and drinking do such great things? Certainly not just eating and drinking do these things, but the words written here: "Given and shed for you for the forgiveness of sins." These words, along with the bodily eating and drinking, are the main thing in the Sacrament. Whoever believes these words has exactly what they say: "forgiveness of sins."

. . . .

Once we have received the gift of new life, that life must be sustained. In the same way that God provides food for our physical life, so, too, He provides food for our new life in Christ. Like a caring parent, God gives His children the nourishment they cannot provide for themselves. The body and blood of Christ are food for our souls. The benefit of eating and drinking the body and blood of Christ is that we are refreshed and strengthened in our struggle against sin, death, and the devil.

The catechism teaches us that the Sacrament of the Altar provides forgiveness. The forgiveness we receive in the body and blood of Christ refreshes the burdened soul. It satisfies our hunger for the daily reassurance of forgiveness through Jesus. We, like the disciples at the first Lord's Supper, are fed directly by Jesus. He gives us this gracious gift in order to strengthen us in our struggle against sin and all the forces that oppose us until He comes again. Like the manna given to the Israelites in their desert travels, the Sacrament of the Altar provides us with spiritual food for our earthly journey. The body and blood of Christ is our never-ending sustenance for our journey to the promised land—the new heaven and earth.

This is My blood of the covenant, which is poured out for many for the forgiveness of sins.

(MATTHEW 26:28)

O LIVING BREAD FROM HEAVEN, HOW WELL YOU FEED YOUR GUEST!

THE GIFTS THAT YOU HAVE GIVEN HAVE FILLED MY HEART WITH REST. **(LSB 642:1)**

THE SACRAMENT OF THE ALTAR (PART THREE)

How can you prepare your heart to receive Jesus in His Supper?

Who receives this sacrament worthily? Fasting and bodily preparation are certainly fine outward training. But that person is truly worthy and well prepared who has faith in these words: "Given and shed for you for the forgiveness of sins."

But anyone who does not believe these words or doubts them is unworthy and unprepared, for the words "for you" require all hearts to believe.

. . . .

While the body and blood of Jesus are present in the Sacrament of the Altar regardless of the worthiness of those who administer and receive it, we are called by God to receive it in a worthy way. To receive the body and blood of Christ in a way that it pleasing to God and beneficial for our life, the Sacrament is to be received in faith. Like all gifts from God, the body and blood of Jesus can be received in a way that is beneficial and in a way that is detrimental. Those who partake of the Sacrament without faith in Jesus and His promises are convicted by the body and blood of Christ instead of forgiven and refreshed. It is Jesus' desire that all who join Him at His Table recognize His presence and receive Him in faith.

The catechism teaches us that we are to receive the body and blood of Jesus with a faithful heart—a heart that trusts in God's promises and clings to Jesus who is present in the Sacrament. God has placed His gift of forgiveness on the Table for all to partake. It is His desire that it be received in the joy of forgiveness and the expectation of, and eagerness for, His return.

Let a person examine himself, then, and so eat of the bread and drink of the cup.

(1 CORINTHIANS 11:28)

DAILY PRAYERS

MORNING AND EVENING

What are the possible benefits of beginning and ending your day in prayer?

Luther taught that being a Christian without prayer is like being alive without breathing. Prayer is a vital resource for the Christian's daily life. Prayer enables us to bring our worries to God so we are freed to focus on fulfilling His will. Luther explained that prayer is not our attempt to overcome God's will; instead it is us being open to His willingness to give us the gracious gifts He desires to provide. The power of prayer is something that cannot be fully explained; prayer must be experienced. Prayer comes in many forms. Prayers are spoken, sung, written, and even drawn. Regardless of their form, prayer is a strong medicine for our soul. The following are Luther's prayers for morning and evening:

In the morning when you get up, make the sign of the holy cross and say:

> In the name of the Father and of the + Son and of the Holy Spirit. Amen.

Then, kneeling or standing, repeat the Creed and the Lord's Prayer. If you choose, you may also say this little prayer:

> I thank You, my heavenly Father, through Jesus Christ, Your dear Son, that You have kept me this night from all harm and danger; and I pray that You would keep me this day also from sin and every evil, that all my doings and life may please You. For into Your hands I commend myself, my body and soul, and all things. Let Your holy angel be with me, that the evil foe may have no power over me. Amen.

Then go joyfully to your work, singing a hymn, like that of the Ten Commandments, or whatever your devotion may suggest.

In the evening when you go to bed, make the sign of the holy cross and say:

> In the name of the Father and of the + Son and of the Holy Spirit. Amen.

Then kneeling or standing, repeat the Creed and the Lord's Prayer. If you choose, you may also say this little prayer:

> I thank You, my heavenly Father, through Jesus Christ, Your dear Son, that You have graciously kept me this day; and I pray that You would forgive me all my sins where I have done wrong, and graciously keep me this night. For into Your hands I commend myself, my body and soul, and all things. Let Your holy angel be with me, that the evil foe may have no power over me. Amen.

Then go to sleep at once and in good cheer.

HAVE WE TRIALS AND TEMPTATIONS? IS THERE TROUBLE ANYWHERE?

WE SHOULD NEVER BE DISCOURAGED—TAKE IT TO THE LORD IN PRAYER. **(LSB 770:2)**

MY PRAYERS

MONDAY

....

....

TUESDAY

....

....

WEDNESDAY

....

....

THURSDAY

....

....

FRIDAY

....

....

SATURDAY

....

....

SUNDAY

....

....

THEN GO JOYFULLY TO YOUR WORK . . .

THEN GO TO SLEEP AT ONCE AND IN GOOD CHEER . . .

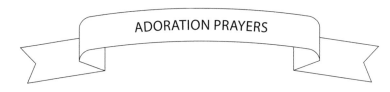

ADORATION PRAYERS

What characteristics of God cause you to give Him praise and adoration?

Prayers of adoration praise God for His unique and gracious character. They highlight aspects of God that set Him apart from all others. Giving God praise is at the heart of Christian worship. It acknowledges that we, His creatures, see His true identity and character. In 1 Chronicles, we are presented with a powerful prayer of adoration.

> Yours, O LORD, is the greatness and the power and the glory and the victory and the majesty, for all that is in the heavens and in the earth is Yours. Yours is the kingdom, O LORD, and You are exalted as head above all. Both riches and honor come from You, and You rule over all. In Your hand are power and might, and in Your hand it is to make great and to give strength to all. **(1 CHRONICLES 29:11–12)**

Prayers of adoration are spoken not only by God's children on earth but also by the company of heaven. In the Book of Revelation, we see the heavenly host surrounding the throne of God shouting prayers of adoration.

> Then I looked, and I heard around the throne and the living creatures and the elders the voice of many angels, numbering myriads of myriads and thousands of thousands, saying with a loud voice, "Worthy is the Lamb who was slain, to receive power and wealth and wisdom and might and honor and glory and blessing!", And I heard every creature in heaven and on earth and under the earth and in the sea, and all that is in them, saying, "To Him who sits on the throne and to the Lamb be blessing and honor and glory and might forever and ever!" And the four living creatures said, "Amen!" and the elders fell down and worshiped. **(REVELATION 5:11–14)**

PRAISE GOD, FROM WHOM ALL BLESSINGS FLOW; PRAISE HIM, ALL CREATURES HERE BELOW;

PRAISE HIM ABOVE, YE HEAV'NLY HOST: PRAISE FATHER, SON, AND HOLY GHOST. AMEN. **(*LSB* 805:1)**

CONFESSION PRAYERS

How can confession strengthen your relationship with God and others?

Prayers of confession express sorrow for our sin and request God's forgiveness and strength to change. While prayers of confession can be difficult, we know that as God's children, forgiveness is given in Jesus Christ. One of the most beautiful examples of a prayer of confession comes from King David.

Have mercy on me, O God,
    according to Your steadfast love;
according to Your abundant mercy
    blot out my transgressions.
Wash me thoroughly from my iniquity,
    and cleanse me from my sin!
For I know my transgressions,
    and my sin is ever before me.
Against You, You only, have I sinned
    and done what is evil in Your sight,
so that You may be justified in Your words
    and blameless in Your judgment.
Behold, I was brought forth in iniquity,
    and in sin did my mother conceive me.

Behold, You delight in truth in the inward
    being,
    and You teach me wisdom in the
      secret heart.
Purge me with hyssop, and I shall be clean;
    wash me, and I shall be whiter than snow.
Let me hear joy and gladness;
    let the bones that You have broken
      rejoice.
Hide Your face from my sins,
    and blot out all my iniquities.
Create in me a clean heart, O God,
    and renew a right spirit within me.
Cast me not away from Your presence,
    and take not Your Holy Spirit from me.
Restore to me the joy of Your salvation,
    and uphold me with a willing spirit.

(PSALM 51:1–12)

LORD, ON YOU I CAST MY BURDEN. SINK IT TO THE DEPTHS BELOW.

LET ME KNOW YOUR GRACIOUS PARDON, WASH ME, MAKE ME WHITE AS SNOW. *(LW 233:4)*

THANKSGIVING PRAYERS

Prayers of thanksgiving acknowledge God for His gifts of grace and love. While prayers of supplication are often more common among Christians, prayers of thanksgiving are the way we express our awareness that God is the source of all blessings even when they come through earthly means. Psalms 136 and 100 encourage us to offer God our thanks.

What blessings has God given you that you are thankful for?

Give thanks to the LORD, for He is good,
    for His steadfast love endures forever.
Give thanks to the God of gods,
    for His steadfast love endures forever.
Give thanks to the Lord of lords,
    for His steadfast love endures forever.

(PSALM 136:1–3)

Make a joyful noise to the LORD, all the earth!
    Serve the LORD with gladness!
    Come into His presence with singing!
Know that the LORD, He is God!
    It is He who made us, and we are His;
    we are His people, and the sheep
        of His pasture.
Enter His gates with thanksgiving,
    and His courts with praise!
    Give thanks to Him; bless His name!
For the LORD is good;
    His steadfast love endures forever,
    and His faithfulness to all generations.

(PSALM 100)

NOW THANK WE ALL OUR GOD WITH HEARTS AND HANDS AND VOICES,

WHO WONDROUS THINGS HAS DONE, IN WHOM HIS WORLD REJOICES. *(LSB 895:1)*

SUPPLICATION PRAYERS

For what anxieties in life do you need God to provide His blessing and grace?

Prayers of supplication are humble requests to God to provide for our needs of body and soul. In the Book of Philippians, we learn that not only are we invited to ask God for all our needs, but also in doing so, our anxiety is turned to peace.

> The Lord is at hand; do not be anxious about anything, but in everything by prayer and supplication with thanksgiving let your requests be made known to God. And the peace of God, which surpasses all understanding, will guard your hearts and your minds in Christ Jesus. **(PHILIPPIANS 4:5B–7)**

In the Book of Ephesians, the apostle Paul makes a request on behalf of the Christians in Ephesus.

> For this reason I bow my knees before the Father, from Whom every family in heaven and on earth is named, that according to the riches of His glory He may grant you to be strengthened with power through His Spirit in your inner being, so that Christ may dwell in your hearts through faith—that you, being rooted and grounded in love, may have strength to comprehend with all the saints what is the breadth and length and height and depth, and to know the love of Christ that surpasses knowledge, that you may be filled with all the fullness of God.

> Now to Him who is able to do far more abundantly than all that we ask or think, according to the power at work within us, to Him be glory in the church and in Christ Jesus throughout all generations, forever and ever. Amen. **(EPHESIANS 3:14–21)**

PENITENT SINNERS, FOR MERCY CRYING, PARDON AND PEACE FROM HIM OBTAIN;

EVER THE WANTS OF THE POOR SUPPLYING, THEIR FAITHFUL GOD HE WILL REMAIN. *(LSB 797:4)*

TABLE OF DUTIES

TABLE OF DUTIES: VOCATION

How does Luther's teaching on vocation change how you view the roles and responsibilities you have been given?

In Luther's original Small Catechism, he provided a variety of Bible passages meant to inform the various roles and occupations of his time. While it was impossible to include every vocation, Luther's underlying principle was the same. Luther taught that our vocations are God's way of providing our neighbors with the good things they need. When a father and mother instruct their children in the ways of the Lord, God is working through them. When a citizen fulfills his civic duty and obeys those placed in authority over him, God is working through him as well. Even when a farmer milks a cow or a carpenter builds a house, it is God who is providing the milk and the home. Faithfully fulfilling our vocations by serving our neighbors in love is one way God fulfills our neighbor's prayer for daily bread. In his lectures on the Book of Galatians, Luther puts it this way:

> But those who accept the doctrine of faith and, in accordance with this commandment of Paul's, love one another do not criticize someone else's way of life and works; but each one approves the way of life of another and the duties which the other performs in his vocation. No godly person believes that the position of a magistrate is better in the sight of God than that of a subject, for he knows that both are divine institutions and have a divine command behind them. He will not distinguish between the position or work of a father and that of a son, or between that of a teacher and that of a pupil, or between that of a master and that of a servant; but he will declare it as certain that both are pleasing to God if they are done in faith and in obedience to God. In the eyes of the world, of course, these ways of life and their positions are unequal; but this outward inequality does not in any way hinder the unity of spirit, in which they all think and believe the same thing about Christ, namely, that through Him alone we obtain the forgiveness of sins and righteousness. As for outward behavior and position in the world, one person does not judge another or criticize his works or praise his own, even if they are superior; but with one set of lips and one spirit they confess that they have one and the same Savior, Christ, before whom there is no partiality toward either persons or works. **(AE 27:60–61)**

THEE MAY I SET AT MY RIGHT HAND, WHOSE EYES MY INMOST SUBSTANCE SEE, AND LABOR ON AT THY COMMAND, AND OFFER ALL MY WORKS TO THEE. *(LSB 854:3)*

THE THREE SOLAS

The three solas summarize the three basic principles of the Reformation. We are saved by grace alone; grace is received through faith alone; and faith is given by the Holy Spirit through Scripture alone. The following pages contain quotes from Luther and Bible passages you can use to reflect on the three solas.

SOLA GRATIA

SOLA FIDE

SOLA SCRIPTURA

GRACE ALONE

SOLA GRATIA

God has not rejected His people whom He foreknew. Do you not know what the Scripture says of Elijah, how he appeals to God against Israel? "Lord, they have killed Your prophets, they have demolished Your altars, and I alone am left, and they seek my life." But what is God's reply to him? "I have kept for Myself seven thousand men who have not bowed the knee to Baal." So too at the present time there is a remnant, chosen by grace. But if it is by grace, it is no longer on the basis of works; otherwise grace would no longer be grace.

(ROMANS 11:2–6)

WHOEVER DOES NOT RECEIVE SALVATION PURELY THROUGH GRACE, INDEPENDENTLY OF ALL GOOD WORKS, CERTAINLY WILL NEVER RECEIVE IT OTHERWISE. **(LUTHER, AE 75:238)**

FAITH ALONE

SOLA FIDE

But now the righteousness of God has been manifested apart from the law, although the Law and the Prophets bear witness to it—the righteousness of God through faith in Jesus Christ for all who believe. For there is no distinction: for all have sinned and fall short of the glory of God, and are justified by His grace as a gift, through the redemption that is in Christ Jesus, whom God put forward as a propitiation by His blood, to be received by faith... For we hold that one is justified by faith apart from works of the law. **(ROMANS 3:21–25A, 28)**

IN MY HEART THERE RULES THIS ONE DOCTRINE, NAMELY, FAITH IN CHRIST. FROM IT, THROUGH IT, AND TO IT ALL MY THEOLOGICAL THOUGHT FLOWS AND RETURNS, DAY AND NIGHT. **(LUTHER, AE 27:145)**

SCRIPTURE ALONE

SOLA SCRIPTURA

But as for you, continue in what you have learned and have firmly believed, knowing from whom you learned it and how from childhood you have been acquainted with the sacred writings, which are able to make you wise for salvation through faith in Christ Jesus. All Scripture is breathed out by God and profitable for teaching, for reproof, for correction, and for training in righteousness, that the man of God may be complete, equipped for every good work.

(2 TIMOTHY 3:14–17)

THINK OF THE SCRIPTURES AS THE LOFTIEST AND NOBLEST OF HOLY THINGS,

AS THE RICHEST OF MINES WHICH CAN NEVER BE SUFFICIENTLY EXPLORED. **(LUTHER, AE 35:235)**

The Luther rose is the most well-known symbol of Lutheranism. Here is how Martin Luther explained it: First, there is a **black cross** in a **heart that remains its natural color**. This is to remind me that it is faith in the Crucified One that saves us. Anyone who believes from the heart will be justified (Romans 10:10). It is a black cross, which mortifies and causes pain, but it leaves the heart its natural color. It doesn't destroy nature, that is to say, it does not kill us but keeps us alive, for the just shall live by faith in the Crucified One (Romans 1:17). The heart should stand in the middle of a white rose. This is to show that faith gives joy, comfort, and peace—it puts the believer into a white, joyous rose. Faith does not give peace and joy like the world gives (John 14:27). This is why the **rose must be white**, not red. White is the color of the spirits and angels (cf. Matthew 28:3; John 20:12). **This rose should stand in a sky-blue field**, symbolizing that a joyful spirit and faith is a beginning of heavenly, future joy, which begins now, but is grasped in hope, not yet fully revealed. Around the field of blue is **a golden ring** to symbolize that blessedness in heaven lasts forever and has no end. Heavenly blessedness is exquisite, beyond all joy and better than any possessions, just as gold is the most valuable and precious metal.